To Michèle Isvy
T. C.

A character by Thierry Courtin

Édition originale française: T'choupi visite Paris

92 avenue de avenue France, 75013 Paris

92 avenue de France, 75013 Paris
Traduction : Eva Grynszpan

ISBN : 978-2-09-503401-6
Loi n°49-956 du 16 juillet 1949
sur les publications destinées à la jeunesse,
modifiée par la loi n°2011-525 du 17 mai 2011.

Ce livre est imprimé sur du papier issu de forêts gérées durablement.

Achevé d'imprimer en janvier 2024 par Pollina, Luçon, France.
N° d'éditeur : 374673/ 10296784 - Dépôt légal : mars 2024

T'choupi

in Paris

Illustrated by Thierry Courtin

Nathan

Daddy, Mommy and T'choupi are spending their holidays in Paris.
"Look T'choupi, it's **the Eiffel Tower**!" says Daddy.
"Can we climb to the top?"
"Sure, but there are 674 steps. If you want, we can take the elevator."

Now, let's go to **the Louvre Museum**!
"Daddy, will you take my picture in front of the Pyramid?"

Many different works of art are shown at the museum.
There are famous paintings like **the Mona Lisa**,
and very impressive sculptures!

Up on the bridge,
T'choupi counts
the Bateaux-Mouches
sailing on the Seine river.

Then he spots strange monsters at the top of **the Notre-Dame cathedral**...

"These are gargoyles," Mommy explains.

"They are used to drain the rainwater away."

Traveling in Paris is easy with **the métro**.
"It's like a train, but it goes underground," says Mommy.

This tour is quite exhausting!
T'choupi and his parents take a break at **a café**.

"Hello, an orange juice for my dad, a coffee for my mom and a lemonade for me, please," T'choupi asks the waiter.

Here we go again! Daddy, Mommy and T'choupi take **the funicular** right to the top of **the Montmartre hill**.

T'choupi marvels at the artists painting in **the Place du Tertre**.

Then he takes a ride on the **merry-go-round**.
"Hi Daddy!"

It's lunchtime! The family has a picnic in front of **the Sacré-Cœur Basilica**.

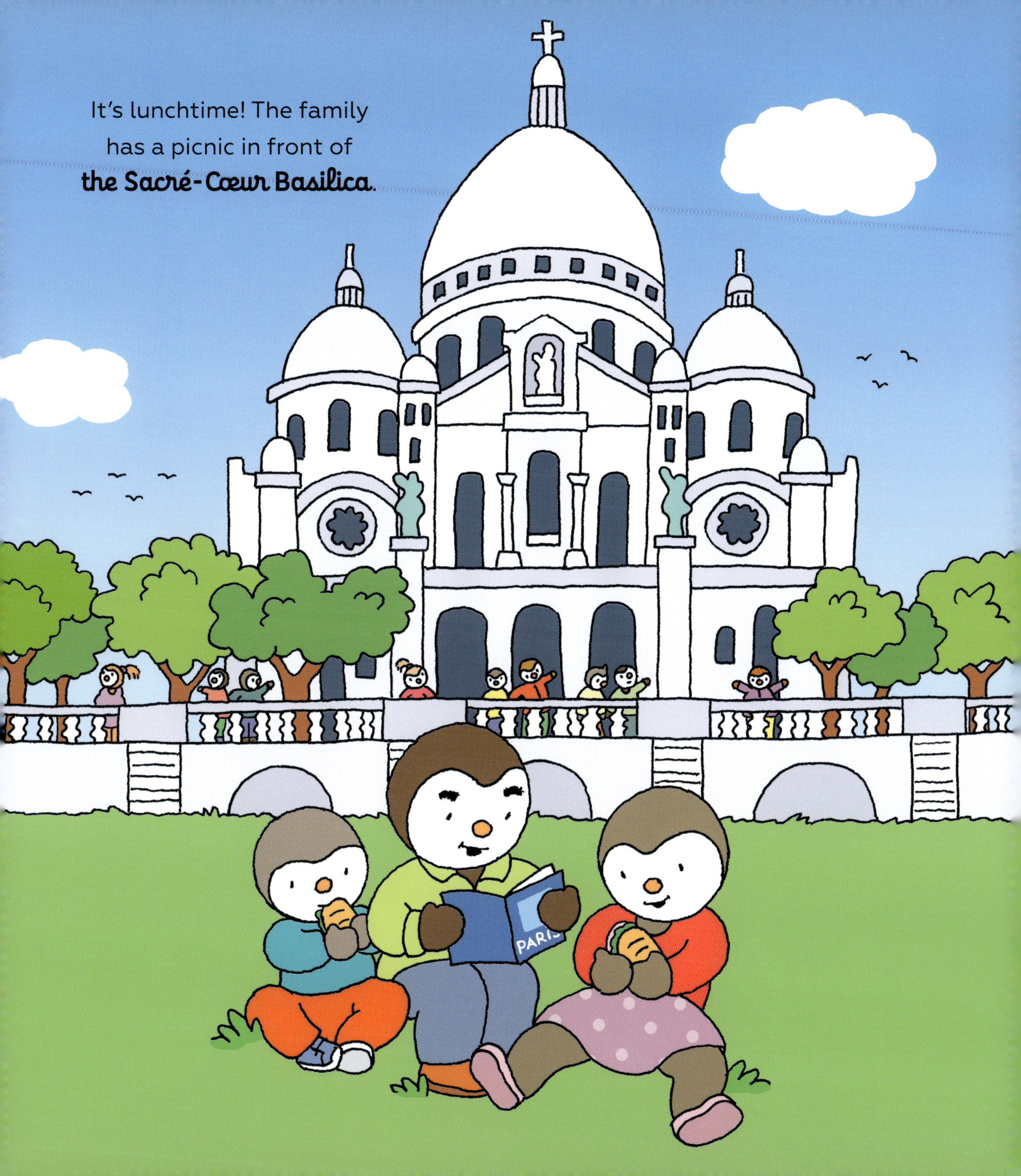

And there's more! At the top of **the Champs-Élysées** avenue stands **the Arc de Triomphe**. What a sight!

As T'choupi walks down the avenue, he sees so many **shops**!
"Can we buy a souvenir for Grandpa and Grandma?" he asks.

It’s nice to rest at
the Luxembourg Garden
after such a crowd!

On a large pond, **the Grand Bassin**,
T’choupi sends a model boat to sail.

He rides the cutest **pony**,

and even sees
a **puppet** show!

At the **National Museum of Natural History**, real dinosaur skeletons are displayed! But T'choupi's favorite is the **Grand Gallery of Evolution**. There are so many animals to look at!

"Can you spot all those from Africa?" asks Daddy.

Later on, T'choupi arrives at a funny-looking building made with huge pipes.
It's **the Pompidou Center**.

It’s full of amazing paintings and sculptures!

Their last stop is at **the Garnier Opera**.

"Let's see a ballet tonight," suggest Mommy and Daddy.

At the end of the show, T'choupi claps loudly.
"Bravo! What a wonderful holiday in **Paris**!"

MY MAP OF PARIS

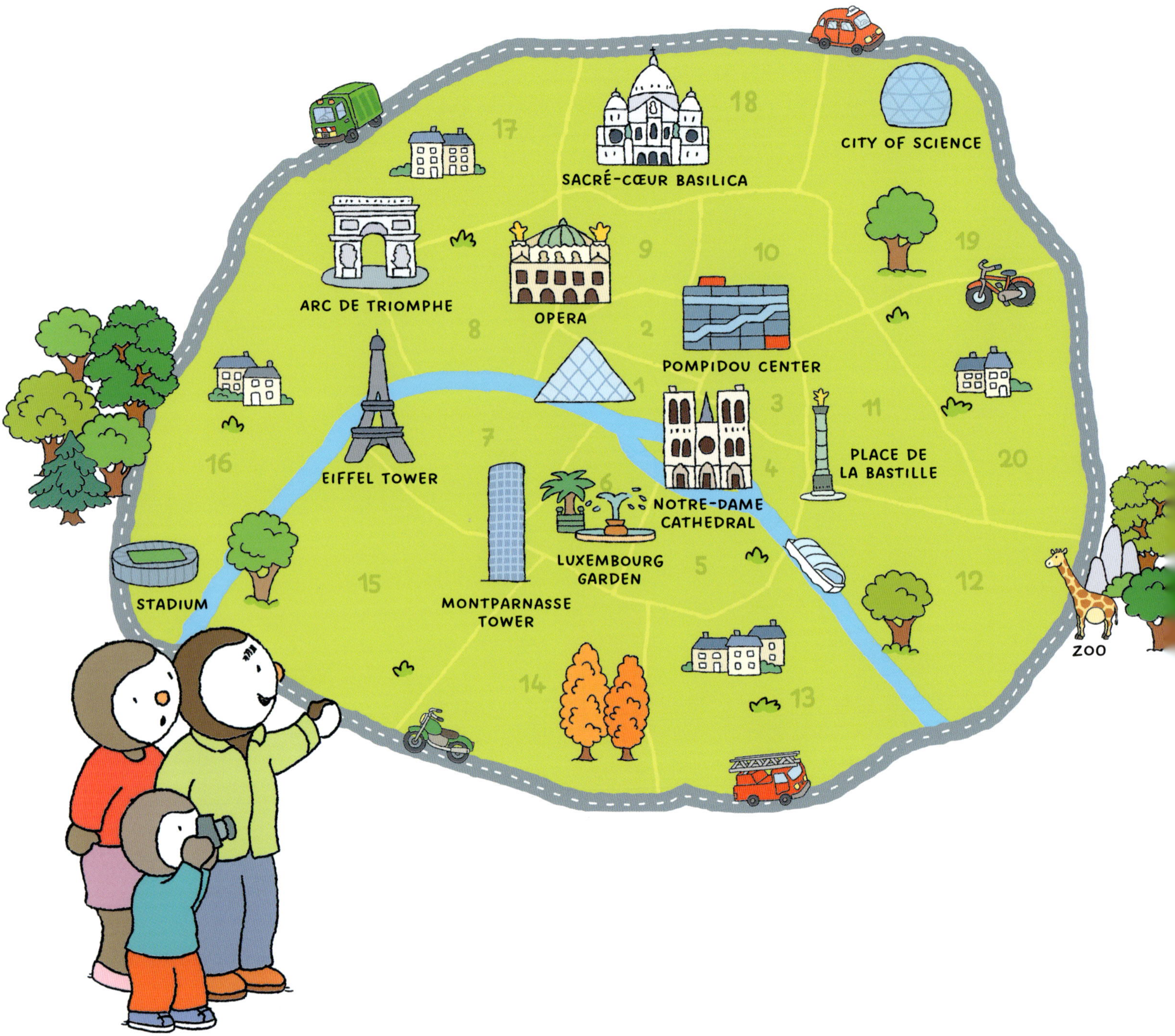